How Do I Use Social Networking?

Tricia Yearling

How Do I Use Social Networking?

Online Smarts

Tricia Yearling

Enslow Publishing
101 W. 23rd Street
Suite 240
New York, NY 10011
USA

enslow.com

Words to Know

cyberbully—A person who scares, embarrasses, or hurts someone else online.

icon—A picture that stands for something on a computer.

membership—Being a member of something.

password—A secret combination of letters or numbers that lets someone enter something.

predator—A person who looks for and harms other people.

profile—The identity that a social network user sets up online.

social network—An online community where members can share information and play games.

username—The name a person uses on a computer.

Contents

Connecting Online

Are you a member of Whyville or Moshi Monsters? Do you have an Everloop account? You may not know the term *social network*, but if you have spent time on one of these sites, you're a part of one! Social networks are online communities where people play games, talk to friends, share news, and give their opinions about movies, TV shows, singers, and sports. These sites let you communicate with family and friends around the world.

Social networks are on the Internet. To access them, all you need is a computer, tablet, or cell phone with an Internet connection. Used safely, online social networks can be lots of fun. They let you use your imagination and help you connect with people.

Games, Messages, and More

Many kids use online social networks, such as Moshi Monsters and Whyville, to play games. Some games help teach reading and math and others teach problem solving. And some games allow users to play in a made-up world. In WeeWorld, users create a WeeMee, an avatar to use in

SAFETY TIP!

Limit yourself to no more than two hours of time online each day.

On Moshi Monsters, kids can adopt pet monsters, explore Monster City, play games, and do puzzles.

WeeWorld. Users can then design their WeeMee's room, chat with friends, and play games.

Many of the games on social-networking sites are played alone. Multiplayer games are played by large groups of people.

But networking sites offer more than just games. Social networks, such as Everloop, allow users to post stories, send messages, and learn to connect with people using a computer. These activities can teach you to be responsible online.

SAFETY TIP! Do not sign up for an online account without an adult's permission.

Multiplayer games allow many people to play together. Even people from around the world can play together online.

Learning Your Way Around

Online social networks are communities. When you sign up for a social network, you start a **membership**. As a member, you can access the site's features. Look around to see what is there. Try some of the games. Watch how people using the site talk to each other. Ask yourself, "How can I use this site?" Try different sites to see which ones you like best.

SAFETY TIP!

Ask your friends for tips on which social-networking sites to check out.

Signing On

Carefully choose the social networks you use. Some, like Whyville and Grom Social, are specifically for kids in elementary and middle school. Others, like Instagram and Facebook, are for teenagers or adults. You must be at least thirteen years old to join. Never pretend to be older online than you really are. Age minimums are there to keep kids safe.

Talk with a parent before you sign up for a social network. She can help you decide if it is right for you. For example, Grom Social is a social network for kids

SAFETY TIP!

Spend time checking out a site before you sign up. Make sure it is right for you.

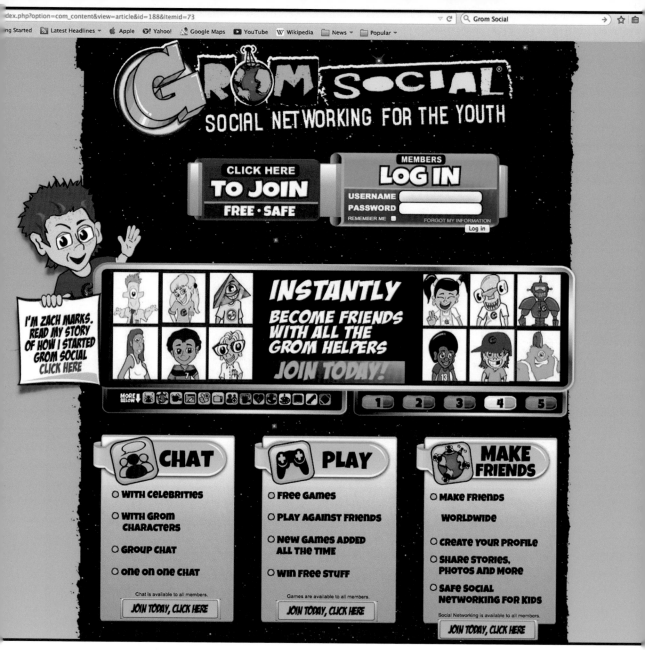

Grom Social was created by a kid for kids so they have a fun, safe place to go to.

between the ages of five and sixteen. An eleven-year-old boy created it because he was too young to use Facebook. It's kid-friendly and bully-free. No matter how old you are, there is a safe, fun social network for you and your interests.

Pick a social networking site that is right for your age and your interests.

Follow the Rules

To join most online social networks, you will have to give an e-mail address where the site can send you messages to start your membership. Many networking sites ask you to pick a **password** and **username**. Do not use your real name. Everyone on a site can see usernames.

Always check out a social-networking site with an adult before you join it. Have the adult read and explain the site's rules, or terms of use, so that you know what is allowed. If you see anyone

breaking these rules, block that person or report him to the site. Find out where to get help on the site in case you forget your password or have other problems.

Creating Your Online Profile

Most sites let you set limits on whom you can chat with and what you can do. Some sites let you chat by typing your own words while others require you to pick from a list of common phrases.

Many online social networks let you set up a **profile**. This is a page where you tell people about yourself. It is important to make good,

Ask a parent to explain the rules of the social networking site you want to sign up for so you know how you and others should behave while on it.

safe choices here. Rather than using a photo of yourself online, choose a picture of an object or an **icon** for your profile. Do not enter facts about yourself such as your age, phone number, home address, or school. Use other kinds of information instead, such as an activity you like to do or your favorite number. When you are done setting up your profile, make sure that only the people you select can see your profile.

Share Wisely

When you join a social network, other people can see the information that you share. Only post information or photos that you are comfortable with other people seeing. Once you have posted something online, you can't take it back. Even if you delete it, someone may have already downloaded it, forwarded it, or shared it with others.

Be careful about what you share online. Once you post something on the Internet, everyone can see it.

If you are using a site that allows you to type in your own words, be polite. Using all capital letters, bold fonts, or many exclamation points are the online version of yelling. No one likes to be yelled at. Don't share personal information such as your name, address, or phone number.

SAFETY TIP!

Do not share personal facts online.

Online Bullies

Even if you follow all of a networking site's rules, you may come across a **cyberbully,** or online bully. Cyberbullies are people who send mean messages to other people online to try to scare them. They may write messages that make fun of other people or spread mean, untrue stories about other kids. They may post embarrassing pictures of other people online to make them feel bad. Cyberbullies do not follow the rules of the

Sometimes a cyberbully is a stranger. Other times, it may be someone you know from school. Either way, tell an adult.

networking site. Understanding how an online bully works will help you to deal with one.

If an online bully bothers you, or you see a cyberbully picking on someone else, do not answer or talk to the bully. Instead, ask a trusted adult to help you send a message to the site administrator explaining what you saw. If you have not yet had trouble with bullies, plan ahead. Learn how to report bullies. Then you will know what to do if trouble starts!

SAFETY TIP!

If someone puts your personal facts online, tell an adult right away. Have that adult contact the site to remove the information.

Online Predators

Online **predators** are people who try to trick kids into thinking they are their friends. Then these people ask kids to do things that make them feel

Do not share information or chat with people you don't know in real life. Strangers could be online predators.

uncomfortable, that are wrong, or that are against the law.

To avoid online predators, chat online only with people you know in real life. If someone whom you met online asks you how old you are or where you live, do not respond. Never agree to meet in person someone whom you have met online. If you think that a predator is trying to reach you, tell an adult you trust. A parent, teacher, or guardian would be a good person to talk to. This adult may need to get in touch with the police. The police know how to deal with predators and can help you to stop them.

SAFETY TIP!

Report online predators right away.

Signing Off

You may outgrow a social network, or maybe none of your friends use it. You may decide that you want to leave the network. You will need to close your account. Some sites ask people who want their profiles erased to fill out a form. Other sites end memberships for anyone who has not used the site for ninety days. Check your e-mail after asking to end a membership. You may need to take more steps to finish the job. If you are not sure how to leave a social network, ask for help from an adult.

If you leave one networking site, you may want to join another. The Internet changes every day. Some social networks become popular and then fade away. New networks pop up regularly. Discovering online social networks, connecting with friends, and building your own community can be fun. No matter what social networks you join, be careful, stay safe, and enjoy what they have to offer.

SAFETY TIP!

Keep passwords to your social-networking accounts to yourself. If someone finds out a password, change it.

Learn More

Books

Cosson, M. J. *The Smart Kid's Guide to Using the Internet.* North Mankato, Minn: The Child's World, 2014.

Linde, Barbara. *Safe Social Networking.* New York: Gareth Stevens Publishing, 2013.

Schwartz, Heather E. *Safe Social Networking.* Mankato, Minn.: Capstone Press, 2013.

Web Sites

commonsensemedia.org/lists/social-networking-for-kids

Provides Internet safety tips.

netsmartz.org/NetSmartzKids/PasswordRap

Advice for creating a strong password.

onguardonline.gov/articles/0012-kids-and-socializing-online

Tips on safely navigating social networks.

Index

Published in 2016 by Enslow Publishing, LLC.
101 W. 23rd Street, Suite 240, New York, NY 10011

Library of Congress Cataloging-in-Publication Data
Yearling, Tricia.
 How do I use social networking? / Tricia Yearling.
    pages cm. — (Online smarts)
 Includes bibliographical references and index.
 Summary: "Discusses how kids can safely use social networking"—Provided by publisher.
 Audience: 8-up.
 Audience: Grade 4 to 6.
 ISBN 978-0-7660-6858-2 (library binding)
 ISBN 978-0-7660-6856-8 (pbk.)
 ISBN 978-0-7660-6857-5 (6-pack)
 1. Online social networks—Juvenile literature. 2. Online etiquette—Juvenile literature. I. Title.
 HM742.Y43 2015
 302.23'1—dc23   2015007456

Printed in the United States of America

To Our Readers: We have done our best to make sure all Web sites in this book were active and appropriate when we went to press. However, the author and the publisher have no control over and assume no liability for the material available on those Web sites or on any Web sites they may link to. Any comments or suggestions can be sent by e-mail to customerservice@enslow.com.

Photo Credits: Compassionate Eye Foundation/Digial Vision/Getty Images, p. 3 (girl); Elena Kalistratova/ iStock/Thinkstock (chapter opener and front and back matter); Laurence Mouton/PhotoAlto Agency RF Collections/Getty Images, p. 13; Maxiphoto/E+/Getty Images, p. 21; Peter Dazeley/The Image Bank/Getty Image, p. 6; Purestock/Thinkstock (series logo), p. 3; Rach27/iStock/Thinkstock, p. 3 (internet icons); Shouoshu/iStock/Thinkstock (digital background), p. 3; Sashatigar/iStock/Thinkstock (doodle art on contents page and fact boxes); suzieleakey/iStock/Thinkstock, p. 5; Tanya Constantine/Blend Images/Getty Images, p. 16; Visage/Stockbyte/Getty Images; p. 19.

Cover Credit: Compassionate Eye Foundation/Digial Vision/Getty Images (girl); Purestock/Thinkstock (series logo); Shouoshu/iStock/Thinkstock (digital background); Rach27/iStock/Thinkstock (internet icons).